Turner (Runette) v. Thompson (Ronnie) U.S. Supreme Court Transcript of Record with Supporting Pleadings

Floyd M Buford, LAWTON MILLER

Turner (Runette) v. Thompson (Ronnie)
Petition / Floyd M Buford / 1969 / 1411 / 398 U.S. 937 / 90 S.Ct. 1839 / 26 L.Ed.2d 269 / 4-10-1970
Turner (Runette) v. Thompson (Ronnie)
Brief in Opposition (P) / LAWTON MILLER / 1969 / 1411 / 398 U.S. 937 / 90 S.Ct. 1839 / 26 L.Ed.2d 269 / 5-14-1970

Turner (Runette) v. Thompson (Ronnie) U.S.
Supreme Court Transcript of Record with
Supporting Pleadings

Table of Contents

IN THE

Supreme Court of the United States

October Term, 1970

No. 1411

RUNETTE TURNER,

Petitioner,

versus

RONNIE THOMPSON, ET AL,

Respondents.

PETITION FOR WRIT OF CERTIORARI
TO THE UNITED STATES COURT OF
APPEALS FOR THE FIFTH CIRCUIT

BYRD, GROOVER & BUFORD
Floyd M. Buford
165 First Street
Macon, Georgia

ADAMS, O'NEAL, THORNTON,
HEMINGWAY & McKENNEY
Manley F. Brown
549 Mulberry Street
Macon, Georgia
Attorneys for Petitioner

INDEX

TABLE OF AUTHORITIES

Cases:

AUTHORITIES (Continued)

IN THE
SUPREME COURT OF THE UNITED STATES
October Term, 1970

No. _____

RUNETTE TURNER,

Petitioner,

versus

RONNIE THOMPSON, ET AL,

Respondents.

PETITION FOR WRIT OF CERTIORARI TO THE
UNITED STATES COURT OF APPEALS FOR THE
FIFTH CIRCUIT

To the Honorable Chief Justice and Associate Justices
of the Supreme Court of the United States:

Your Petitioner, Runette Turner, respectfully shows:

OPINION BELOW

The opinion below was rendered in *Runette Turner
v. Ronnie Thompson, et al,* _____ F. 2d, _____ (5th Cir.
1970), Docket No. 28510 Summary Calendar (Feb. 9,
1970). A copy of said opinion is appended hereto as
Appendix "A".

STATEMENT OF JURISDICTION

The judgment of the United States Court of Appeals
for the Fifth Circuit was rendered and entered on February 9, 1970.

A Petition for Rehearing was denied by the United States Court of Appeals for the Fifth Circuit on March 10, 1970. Within ninety days thereafter this petition was filed.

The jurisdiction of this Court to review the judgment in this case is conferred by 28 U.S.C. § 1254(1) in that Petitioner is a party to this civil case wherein the United States Court of Appeals for the Fifth Circuit has rendered a judgment adverse to her position.

QUESTIONS PRESENTED FOR REVIEW

I.

Can a municipality constitutionally withdraw, reconsider or revoke an outstanding license for the retail sale of package beer without affording the licensee any notice or opportunity to be present at the hearing at the time the license was withdrawn, reconsidered or revoked?

II.

Does the classification of an appeal as frivolous under Rule 38 Federal Rules of Appellate Procedure and the taxation of costs and attorneys' fees pursuant thereto, when said appeal is based upon a clear line of undisturbed Appellate Judicial Authority, amount to such a denial of free access to the Courts of the United States as to justify the exercise of this Court's supervisory authority to correct such action?

CONSTITUTIONAL PROVISIONS — STAT-
UTES — ORDINANCES — REGULATIONS AND
RULES INVOLVED

I.

The Fourteenth Amendment to the Constitution of
the United States provides:

"Section (1). All persons born or naturalized
in the United States, and subject to the jurisdiction thereof, are citizens of the United States
and of the State wherein they reside. No State
shall make or enforce any law which shall a-
bridge the privileges or immunities of citizens
of the United States; nor shall any State de-
prive any person of life, liberty, or property,
without due process of law; nor deny to any
person within its jurisdiction the equal protection of the laws."

II.

28 U.S.C. § 1343 provides as follows:

"The district courts shall have original jurisdiction of any civil action authorized by law to
be commenced by any person: (4) to recover
damages or to secure equitable or other relief
under any act of Congress providing for the
protection of civil rights, including the right to
vote."

42 U.S.C. §1983 provides as follows:

"Every person who, under color of any statute, ordinance, regulation, custom, or usage, of any state or territory, subjects, or causes to be subjected, any citizen of the United States or other person within the jurisdiction thereof to the deprivation of any rights, privileges, or immunities secured by the Constitution and Laws, shall be liable to the party injured in an action at law, suit in equity, or other proper proceeding for redress."

III.

The Code of Ordinances of the City of Macon, Georgia, provides at page 191 as follows:

"Sec. 2-17.   Reconsideration.

Before the minutes of any previous meeting of council are confirmed, any member may call for a reconsideration of the action of council relative to the same, and such business shall be first in order."

IV.

The Regulations of the City of Macon in the form of a "Policy" relating to licensing of retail beer outlets are appended hereto as Appendix "B". There is no official source to which a citation can be noted.

V.

Rule 38 of the Federal Rules of Appellate Procedure reads as follows:

"If a court of appeals shall determine that an appeal is frivolous, it may award just damages and single or double cost to the Appellee."

STATEMENT OF THE CASE

Mrs. Runette Turner, petitioner, filed an application for a retail package beer license with the City of Macon, Georgia, on April 28, 1969. (R-29). Simultaneously therewith she tendered a check for $187.50 to cover the cost of the license which was accepted by the city. (R-30-31). Petitioner's license was duly approved by the Chief of Police and the Alcohol Control Committee of City Council. (R-10, 18, 30-31). On May 6, 1969, the application was duly approved by Mayor and Council and the license was issued to petitioner on May 7, 1969. (R-10, 18, 31-32) After securing the city license, petitioner obtained the necessary state license at a cost of $25.00. She then obtained a stock of packaged beer at a cost of $198.51. (R-32). Some alterations in her place of business (Five Points Grocery) were necessary before she was able to begin business. (R-32-33). She actually began fully operating under the license on May 8, 1969. (R-33). Later on in the week petitioner heard a rumor that a petition was being circulated in the neighborhood to keep her from selling beer. (R-33). On the following Tuesday, she called City Hall and talked to the City Clerk about the rumor. He assured her that there was nothing to be concerned about "because once a license was issued they very seldom revoked it unless you did something to make them revoke it." (R-33-34). Mrs. Turner received no notice that her license would come up for reconsideration at the Tuesday, May 13, 1969, Council Meeting. (R-34) She was not advised of any charges against her and knew nothing about the upcoming action. (R-34) At the Council Meeting on May 13, 1969, (which petitioner heard by radio) (R-30, 31, 34) some residents of the area where petitioner's place of business was located came to Council Meeting with a petition against her license. (R-34) Petitioner's license was accordingly rescinded at the beginning of Council Meeting. (R-34) Someone was dispatched immediately to pick up the license and it was removed from petitioner's place of business before Council Meeting was over. (R-35) Petitioner's check for the license was deposited by the city the same day her license was revoked. (R-35) Since the removal of the license, petitioner's business has decreased sharply. (R-36) She is in competition with another grocery store about one hundred yards away which has a license. (R-36) After her license was revoked, petitioner was able to get three hundred fifty-one names from the neighborhood on the petition favoring her license. (R-37) Petitioner cannot continue her business without her license. (R-39)

The petitioner filed a complaint under 28 U.S.C. § 1343 and 42 U.S.C. § 1983, alleging a denial of procedural due process in the revocation of her license without the benefit of notice and the right to be heard. The defendants admitted in their answer that "Plaintiff complied with all the requirements for issuance of said license." (R 9-18)

The City of Macon has a "Statement of Policy" concerning malt beverage licenses (R-7-9) and it contains a section on "Revocation". Part IV, Section 4 reads as follows:

> "No license shall be revoked and no bond shall be forfeited unless the licensee has been given at least three (3) days written notice in person or by registered mail of the intention of the committee to recommend such action. Such notice shall specify the time, place and purpose of hearing and statement of charges upon which the committee proposes to take action. At such hearings conducted by the committee the licensee shall have the right to appear in person and by attorney, and both the committee and licensee shall have the right to present evidence under oath, cross-examine witnesses and generally present evidence relating to the question as to whether or not a violation, as set forth in Section 1, Part IV, has occurred, as well as evidence relating to any extenuating or mitigating circumstances. (R-9-10).

Respondents admit that petitioner received no notice of the impending revocation of her license. (R-19-20)

There is a city ordinance 2-17 which the Respondents relied upon in the trial Court to justify their action along with the fact that residents of the petitioner's area had not received notice of Mrs. Turner's application in the newspaper. (R-20-25)

The District Court found for the defendants. (R-72-74) Final judgment was entered from which petitioner seasonably appealed. (R-75-76)

The Court of Appeals for the Fifth Circuit placed this case on the Summary Calendar and affirmed the decision of the trial Court. (R-103-105) The appeal was further determined to be frivolous and costs and attorneys' fees were taxed against appellant. Petitioner's petition for rehearing was denied on March 10, 1970. (R-106)

ARGUMENT

I.

THE DECISION OF THE UNITED STATES COURT OF APPEALS FOR THE FIFTH CIRCUIT IN THIS CASE IS IN CONFLICT WITH DECISIONS BY THE COURT OF APPEALS FOR THE DISTRICT OF COLUMBIA CIRCUIT ON THE SAME MATTER AND IS FURTHER CONTRARY TO APPLICABLE PRINCIPLES OF PROCEDURAL DUE PROCESS AS LAID DOWN BY DECISIONS OF THIS COURT

The decision in the instant case is grounded upon the conclusion that the petitioner failed to show a denial of procedural due process. The trial Court's suggestion of a jurisdictional question was ignored by the Court of Appeals and is not involved in the present posture of the case.

Precisely the same issue involved in the instant case was before the District of Columbia Circuit in the case of *In Re Carter*, 177 F. 2d 75 (D.C. Cir. 1949). That decision repudiated an attempt to return a license, already issued, to a pending status because of facts which, if originally known, would have called for further investigation. The license in the present case was recalled or revoked because the city had failed originally to give public notice of its pendency in the newspaper. The trial Court and the Court of Appeals have found that the city was willing to give petitioner another hearing on a pending application. One quote from *Carter* demonstrates the constitutional deficiency in this reasoning and the conflict between the decision in this case and in *Carter*.

> "The District Court believed that it could return an application to a pending status after a permit had been issued, solely because the Court later learned of circumstances which, if originally known, would have caused it to make further inquiry upon the original application. This it cannot do, any more in this case than in an admission to The Bar or in respect to other forms of outstanding business licenses."

> "We hold that when an authorization to engage in the bonding business has been approved by the District Court and is outstanding,

it can be revoked, prior to the expiration of its
term, only upon a proceeding which contains
the elements of due process of law, i.e., a hearing and revelation of all data upon which a decision is based." 177 F.2d at 78

See also, *Jordan v. United Insurance Company*, 289
F. 2d 778 (D.C. Cir. 1961); *Minkoff v. Payne*, 210 F.
2d 689 (D.C. Cir. 1953).

The decision in the present case is further contrary
to the principles of procedural due process laid down
in *American Trucking Associations v. Frisco Transpor-
tation Company*, 358 U.S. 133, 3 L. 3d. 2d 172 (1958).

The ordinance relied upon by the city to justify its
action is contrary, in its application, to the principle
of *Sniadach v. Family Finance Corp.* ____ U.S. ____,
23 L.2d 2d 349 (1969).

Furthermore, the conclusion reached by the Court
of Appeals is contrary to the teachings of its own cases
regarding procedural due process. See, *Hornsby v. Allen*, 326 F. 2d 605 (5th Cir. 1964); *Crews v. Undercofler*,
371 F. 2d 534 (5th Cir. 1967); *Russell v. Newman Mfg*,
370 F. 2d 980 (5th Cir. 1966).

In effect, the Court of Appeals has held that munici-
pal licensing procedures are completely free from procedural due process requirements. This is not the law,
and such a decision, which invites arbitrary action
and abusive tactics, should not be allowed to stand.

II.

THE CLASSIFICATION OF THIS CASE AS
FRIVOLOUS BY THE COURT OF APPEALS
AND THE TAXATION OF COSTS AND AT-
TORNEY'S FEES AGAINST PETITIONER IS
TANTAMOUNT TO DENIAL OF FREE AC-
CESS TO THE FEDERAL COURTS AND DE-
MANDS THE EXERCISE OF THIS COURT'S
SUPERVISORY POWER TO CORRECT SUCH
ACTION

Petitioner's position in the trial Court was grounded
upon the authorities set out above. No cases appear
to the contrary and even the decisions of the Fifth
Circuit encourage such litigation. The Court now apparently repudiates any effort to bring a licensing case
before it and use the vehicle of financial retribution
and professional embarrassment to accomplish this
end. In the final analysis petitioner has been punished
and counsel humiliated because of reliance upon precedent. Such treatment is contrary to the American ideal
of justice and fair play and is sufficient intimidation
to prevent a prudent attorney from pursuing what appears to be a meritorious cause of action fully sup-
ported by precedent.

We submit that the judgment of the Court of Appeals should be reversed and that petitioner should
be relieved from payment of costs and attorneys' fees.

CONCLUSION

For the reasons stated above, the petition for writ of certiorari should be granted.

Respectfully submitted,

BYRD, GROOVER
& BUFORD

P. O. Address:
165 First Street
Macon, Georgia

_____

Floyd M. Buford
ADAMS, O'NEAL,
THORNTON, HEMINGWAY
& McKENNEY

P. O. Address:
549 Mulberry Street
Macon, Georgia

_____

Manley F. Brown
Attorneys for Petitioner

APPENDIX "A"

IN THE
UNITED STATES COURT OF APPEALS
FOR THE FIFTH CIRCUIT

No. 28510
Summary Calendar

RUNETTE TURNER,
Plaintiff-Appellant,

versus

RONNIE THOMPSON, ET AL.,
Defendants-Appellees.

Appeal from the United States District Court for the
Middle District of Georgia

(February 9, 1970)

Before BROWN, Chief Judge, MORGAN and CLARK,
Circuit Judges.

PER CURIAM: Pursuant to Rule 18 of the Rules
of this Court, we have concluded on the merits that
this case is of such character as not to justify oral

argument and have directed the clerk to place the case on the Summary Calendar and to notify the parties in writing. See *Murphy v. Houma Well Service*, 409 F.2d 804, (5th Cir. 1969), Part I, and *Huth v. Southern Pacific Company*, 417 F.2d 526 (5th Cir. 1969), Part I.

This action was brought against the Mayor and Aldermen of the City of Macon, Georgia to redress an alleged deprivation of civil rights. Plaintiff invoked the jurisdiction of the court below pursuant to 28 U.S.C.A. § 1343 and 42 U.S.C.A. § 1983. In her complaint Plaintiff alleged that the City of Macon issued a license authorizing the retail sale of beer in her grocery store and that one week later defendants, without notice or a hearing, rescinded and revoked her license solely because of a neighborhood protest. The prayer of the complaint sought declaratory judgment and injunctive relief.

On answer and after a full evidentiary hearing the court below, in an incisive opinion appended hereto, found Plaintiff completely failed to show a denial of procedural due process. We agree and affirm.

We would only add that at the time of the actions complained of the City of Macon had a valid subsisting ordinance permitting reconsideration of prior council action in the manner followed here[1] and that the

---

[1]This ordinance provided:
"Sec. 2-17. Reconsideration.
'Before the minutes of any previous meeting of council are confirmed, any member may call for a reconsideration of the action of council relative to the same, and such business shall be first in order."

usual public notice of the pendency of Plaintiff's application had not been given prior to its approval. This lack of notice obviously worked against a number of interested citizens who wished to protest. In the light of the city's demonstrated willingness to give Plaintiff and all interested parties a hearing, we affirm.

The learned District Judge found the Plaintiff's contentions wholly without merit. We agree.

This appeal is determined to be frivolous. Appellant is assessed with single costs plus the payment of a reasonable fee to counsel for Appellee for services rendered in connection with the appeal. In the event the parties cannot agree as to the amount of such fee, it shall be determined by the court below.

AFFIRMED.

OPINION

BOOTLE, District Judge: This suit was filed by plaintiff pursuant to 28 U.S.C.A. § 1343 and 42 U.S.C.A. § 1983 and seeks to compel the Mayor and Council of the City of Macon, Georgia, to return to her a beer license alleged to have been issued to her but subsequently rescinded without notice or hearing.

After careful consideration of the pleadings and evidence, this court is compelled to find for the defendants.

At the outset this court expresses grave doubt as to the jurisdiction of suits of this type where, as here, there is no allegation as to the jurisdictional amount. While it is true that in suits properly brought under the Civil Rights Act, 28 U.S.C.A. § 1343, 42 U.S.C.A. § 1983, no jurisdictional amount is necessary, it would seem also true that in those cases the right asserted is "inherently incapable of pecuniary valuation." See Justice Stone's concurring opinion in *Hague v. Committee for Industrial Organization*, 307 U.S. 496, 529-532, 83 L.Ed. 1423, 1444-1445 (1939).

Property rights, on the other hand, which are capable of pecuniary evaluation should be left to federal question jurisdiction under 28 U.S.C.A. § 1331. *Holt v. Indiana Manufacturing Company*, 176 U.S 68, 44 L.Ed. 374 (1900).

This distinction was recognized by the Court of Appeals for the Fifth Circuit in the recent case of *Bussie v. Long*, 383 F.2d 766, 769 (1967), where they noted that in such cases as the now famous *Hornsby v. Allen*, 326 F.2d 605 (5th Cir. 1964), the facts indicated that federal question jurisdiction, including jurisdictional amount, was probably also present.

In the instant case there is neither allegation nor evidence that the jurisdictional amount is present. However, since the resolution of this question is not necessary for the disposition of this case it will be pretermitted.

The gravamen of Mrs. Turner's complaint is that she was issued a beer license on May 7, 1969, and that the same was revoked on May 13, 1969, without notice or hearing in regard to the revocation as required by the City ordinance relating to revocation and the constitutional guarantee of procedural due process.

We believe such contentions are wholly without merit.

The record shows that there was no revocation as contemplated by the City ordinance relating to revocations. The minutes of the Council meeting of May 13, 1969, make it clear that only the approval of the license was rescinded pending a full consideration of the facts by the Alcohol Control Committee at public hearing. Indeed, the plaintiff herself testified that Mr. Parker, the Chairman of the Alcohol Control Committee, notified her after May 13, 1969 that a hearing would be held on her application, but it appears that plaintiff chose not to pursue that course in favor of this action.

There is a complete failure to show that Mrs. Turner was denied procedural due process.

Accordingly, this court finds for the defendants in respect to all of plaintiff's prayers.

APPENDIX "B"

STATEMENT OF POLICY OF THE MAYOR AND
COUNCIL OF THE CITY OF MACON, GEORGIA, RE-
LATING TO THE LICENSING AND CONTROL OF
THE SALE OF BEER AND OTHER MALT BEVER-
AGES INSIDE THE CORPORATE LIMITS OF THE
CITY OF MACON; PROVIDING FOR THE ISSUANCE
OF LICENSES AND THE REVOCATION THEREOF;
DEFINING THE DUTIES AND OBLIGATIONS OF
LICENSEES AND OTHER MATTERS RELATING
THERETO:

The following statement of policy recommended by
the Alcohol Control Committee of the Mayor and Council is hereby adopted and from date of adoption shall
serve as standards to be considered in the approval
of licenses and for other purposes.

PART I

DEFINITIONS

A. 'Committee' shall mean the Alcohol Control
Committee of Mayor and Council of the City of Macon.

B. 'City' shall refer to all property located within
the corporate limits of the City of Macon, Georgia.

C. 'Beer' shall be defined to mean malt or fermented beverages made in whole or in part from malt
or any similar fermented beverages provided the same
shall not contain more than six percent (6%) of alco-

hol by volume. The licensing and sale of any beverage containing more than six percent (6%) of alcohol by volume shall be governed in accordance with the policy of the Mayor and Council of the City of Macon relating to liquor licenses.   .

D.   Wherever the word 'his' shall be used it shall be deemed to include his, hers, and/or theirs.

PART II

APPLICANTS AND APPLICATIONS

Section 1

All applicants for beer licenses must be of good character or such persons' application shall not be considered.

Section 2

All applicants for beer licenses must show financial responsibility.

Section 3

No such applicant for a new license who has a criminal record or who has been guilty of violating rules, regulations or laws or policy of the City of Macon or the State of Georgia or any political subdivision thereof, governing the sale of alcoholic beverages shall be granted a license.

Section 4

All applicants for licenses for the sale of beer shall be made in person at the Office of the City Clerk of the City of Macon.

Section 5

Applicants for licenses for sale of beer shall file with such application a personal performance bond in the amount of $500.00; such bond to insure compliance with all laws, rules, regulations and policy of the City of Macon. If the application is approved, said bond shall remain in force so long as the license is valid.

Section 6

All applications for the renewal of licenses for the sale of beer must be filed in person at the Office of the City Clerk between December 1st and December 15th of each year for the succeeding year and the prescribed license fee paid at the time of filing.

Section 7

The Committee and the Mayor and Council may, in their sole discretion, consider any extenuating circumstances which may reflect favorably or unfavorably on the applicant, application, or the proposed location of the business. If, in their judgement, circumstances are such that the granting of the license would not be in the best interest of the general public, such circumstances may be grounds for denying the application.

Section 8

No application for the license for the sale of beer shall be approved hereunder unless the applicant's proposed place of business is located in an area in which the operation of such business is permitted by the regulations of the Macon-Bibb County Planning and Zoning Commission.

Section 9

No application for a license to sell beer at a new location (a location where beer is not presently being sold) may be approved where the proposed location is within 300 feet of a Church, School, or College. In determining compliance with this section the distance shall be determined by measuring in a straight line from the property line of the location nearest to the Church, School, or College to the nearest property line of said Church, School, or College.

Section 10

The making of any statement on an application for license to sell beer which shall be later found to be false shall constitute grounds for revocation of said license.

PART III

LICENSEES

Section 1

No beer may be sold in the City except under a license issued in accordance herewith.

Section 2

No license for the sale of beer shall be assignable or transferable except from one partner to another and in the event that a licensed business is sold or closed, licensee must immediately surrender his license to the Chief of Police.

Section 3

The issuance of a license for the sale of beer hereunder for any calendar year or any portion thereof shall not be deemed to vest the licensee with any right of renewal thereof.

Section 4

No person under the age of 18 years shall sell, dispense or serve beer.

Section 5

No licensee shall sell beer to any person under the age of 21 years, and a licensee shall be held responsible for any such sale made by his employees or others in his licensed establishment. At any time a State Driver's License shall be considered the only legal proof of age which would relieve a person making such a sale from responsibility therefor.

Section 6

No beer shall be sold on Sundays, Election Days, or any other day on which the sale of same may be prohibited by order of the Chief of Police.

Section 7

All holders of a license for the sale of 'packaged beer to go' and/or wine shall separate the stock of beer and wine from other non-alcoholic merchandise by a partition at least five (5) feet in height, or store same in a separate room, so that such stock may be closed off and locked at all times when its sale is prohibited, and the same shall be closed off and locked at such times.

Section 8

No holder of a license for the sale of 'packaged beer to go' shall allow beer to be consumed on his premises and any licensee shall be held responsible for such consumption by his customers.

Section 9

All holders of a license for sale of beer shall keep a copy of this policy on his premises and instruct any persons working there with respect to the terms hereof and each licensee and person selling beer shall at all times be familiar with the terms of this policy.

Section 10

The business premises of the holder of a license for the sale of beer, including out-buildings, shall be open to inspection at any and all times by officers or officials authorized to conduct such inspections.

Section 11

The holder of any license for the sale of beer shall post on his beer box or cooler a printed sign, in letters at least four (4) inches high reading as follows: 'Sale of beer to Minors strictly prohibited'.

PART IV

REVOCATION

*Section 1

The performance of any act prohibited herein or the failure to perform any act required hereby, as well as the violation of any Ordinance of the City of Macon or any law, State or Federal, relating to the sale of beer or other alcoholic beverages shall constitute grounds for the revocation of a license.

25

Section 2

A license for the sale of beer may be temporarily suspended and the place of business closed upon receipt of evidence by the Committee from the Chief of Police of any violation referred to in Section 1, Part IV.

Section 3

Any license for the sale of beer issued hereunder may be suspended for a definite length of time, revoked, and/or any part of the entire personal performance bond posted by the licensee forfeited.

Section 4

No license shall be revoked and no bond shall be forfeited unless the licensee has been given at least three (3) days written notice, in person or by registered mail of the intention of the Committee to recommend such action. Such notice shall specify the time, place and purpose of hearing and statement of the charges upon which the Committee proposes to take action. At such hearings conducted by the Committee the licensee shall have the right to appear in person and by attorney, and both the Committee and licensee shall have the right to present evidence under oath, cross-examine witnesses and generally present evidence relating to the question as to whether or not a violation, as set forth in Section 1, Part IV, has occurred, as well as evidence relating to any extenuating or mitigating circumstances.

APPENDIX "C"

UNITED STATES COURT OF APPEALS
FOR THE FIFTH CIRCUIT

October Term, 1969

No. 28510
Summary Calendar

D. C. Docket No. Civ. 2462

RUNETTE TURNER,
Plaintiff-Appellant,

versus

RONNIE THOMPSON, ET AL,
Defendants-Appellees.

Appeal from the United States District Court for the
Middle District of Georgia

Before BROWN, Chief Judge, MORGAN and CLARK,
Circuit Judges.

JUDGMENT

This cause came on to be heard on the transcript
of the record from the United States District Court

for the Middle District of Georgia, and was taken under submission by the Court upon the record and briefs on file, pursuant to rule 18;

ON CONSIDERATION WHEREOF, It is now here ordered and adjudged by this Court that the judgment of the said District Court in this cause be, and the same is hereby, affirmed.

It is further ordered that plaintiff-appellant pay to defendants-appellees, the costs on appeal to be taxed by the Clerk of this Court.

February 9, 1970

Issued as Mandate:

APPENDIX "D"

IN THE
UNITED STATES COURT OF APPEALS
FOR THE FIFTH CIRCUIT

No. 28510
Summary Calendar

RUNETTE TURNER,
                                Plaintiff-Appellant,

versus

RONNIE THOMPSON, ET AL.,
                                Defendants-Appellees.

Appeal from the United States District Court for the
Middle District of Georgia

(March 10, 1970)

ON PETITION FOR REHEARING

Before BROWN, Chief Judge, MORGAN and CLARK,
Circuit Judges.

PER CURIAM: IT IS ORDERED that the petition
for rehearing filed in the above entitled and numbered
cause be and the same is hereby denied.

CERTIFICATE OF SERVICE

This is to certify that I have this day served the foregoing petition for writ of certiorari upon Mr. Gerald Mullis and Mr. Phillip Brown, Counsel of Record for the Respondents by depositing a copy of same in the United States Mail with First Class Postage prepaid and addressed to said Counsel of Record at their Post Office Address at 305 American Federal Building, Macon, Georgia.

This ____ day of _____, 1970.

_____

Floyd M. Buford
Counsel of Record

IN THE

SUPREME COURT OF THE UNITED STATES

OCTOBER TERM, 1969

No. 1411

RUNETTE TURNER,
Petitioner,

v.

RONNIE THOMPSON, et al.,
Respondents.

On Petition for a Writ of Certiorari to the United States
Court of Appeals for the Fifth Circuit

BRIEF FOR THE RESPONDENTS IN OPPOSITION

JOHN B. HARRIS, JR.
1200 Georgia Power Building
Macon, Georgia 31201
Counsel of Record for Respondents

Of Counsel
LAWTON MILLER
501 Georgia Power Building
Macon, Georgia 31201
GERALD S. MULLIS
305 American Federal Building
Macon, Georgia 31201

St. Louis Law Printing Co., Inc., 411-15 N. Eighth St. 63101   314-231-4477

INDEX

IN THE

SUPREME COURT OF THE UNITED STATES

OCTOBER TERM, 1969

No. 1411

RUNETTE TURNER,
Petitioner,

v.

RONNIE THOMPSON, et al.,
Respondents.

On Petition for a Writ of Certiorari to the United States
Court of Appeals for the Fifth Circuit

BRIEF FOR THE RESPONDENTS IN OPPOSITION

OPINIONS BELOW

The opinion of the United States Circuit Court for the Fifth Circuit is reported at 421 F. 2d 771. The opinion of the United States District Court for the Middle District of Georgia is not reported but is set out as an appendix at pages 772 and 773 to the Circuit Court opinion set forth above.

JURISDICTION

The judgment of the Court of Appeals was entered on February 9, 1970, and rehearing was denied on March 10, 1970. The petition for certiorari was filed on April 10, 1970. Respondents were granted pursuant to Rule 34, subparagraph 5, an extension of time through May 20, 1970, to file their brief in opposition. The jurisdiction of this Court is invoked under 28 U. S. C. 1254 (1).

QUESTIONS PRESENTED

I

Where a municipality has an ordinance providing that before the minutes of a previous meeting are confirmed the city council may reconsider such prior action, does the withdrawal pursuant to such ordinance of the prior grant of a beer license to petitioner violate constitutional rights of such petitioner?

II

Does the classification by the Circuit Court pursuant to Rule 38 of the Federal Rules of Appellate Procedure of petitioner's appeal as frivolous call for the exercise of this Court's power of supervision?

STATEMENT OF THE CASE

Petitioner sought and obtained from respondents, the Mayor and City Council of the City of Macon, Georgia, a license to sell package beer at retail in her store (R. 29, 31). This action was taken by respondents at their regular weekly meeting on May 6, 1969 (R. 30, 31).

At the next regular meeting of Mayor and Council on May 13, 1969, it appeared that residents of the neighborhood in which petitioner's store was located had not known of petitioner's application prior to its consideration on May 6, 1969 (R. 53, 54). This was apparently because the notice of such application had not been published in the local newspaper as had been the informal custom at that time (R. 53, 54). Many residents of the neighborhood appeared at the meeting of City Council on May 13, 1969, to protest the sale of beer in the neighborhood (R. 53, 58).

When the neighborhood protest was noted at the meeting on May 13, 1969, respondents invoked the provisions of City Ordinance Section 2-17 as follows:

> "Reconsideration. Before the minutes of any previous meeting of council are confirmed, any member may call for a reconsideration of the action of council relative to the same, and such business shall be first in order" (R. 52, 53, 62, 63).

The grant of the license to petitioner was thus reconsidered and the action of the previous meeting in regard to the license was rescinded (R. 95, 96). The chairman of the Alcohol Control Committee stated that a public hearing would be held on petitioner's application for a beer license (R. 97). This was communicated to petitioner but neither petitioner nor her attorney ever requested that such hearing be held (R. 41, 42). Instead petitioner commenced her action in the United States District Court for the Middle District of Georgia, seeking a declaratory judgment and injunctive relief against respondents (R. 2-15).

A trial on the merits was held before Chief Judge W. A. Bootle, United States District Court for the Middle District of Georgia, on August 26, 1969 (R. 28, et seq.). His opinion finding for respondents was filed September 5, 1969 (R. 72, et seq.). Judgment followed on September 11, 1969 (R. 75). Petitioner appealed to the United States Circuit Court for the Fifth Circuit which affirmed unanimously on February 9, 1970. Rehearing was denied on March 10, 1970.

ARGUMENT

I

Petitioner contends the opinion of the United States Court of Appeals for the Fifth Circuit in the instant case is in conflict with opinions of the United States Court of Appeals for the District of Columbia. She relies primarily on the case of **In re Carter**, 177 F. 2d 75. The **Carter** case stands for the proposition that a mid-term revocation of a bondsman's license cannot be accomplished without a hearing fulfilling the requirements of due process.

In the instant case, however, petitioner's license was not revoked but its grant was reconsidered and rescinded pursuant to the provisions of the ordinance of the City of Macon, Section 2-17, *supra*, pending a public hearing by the Alcohol Control Committee. The ordinance was admitted on the trial in the District Court without objection (R. 68, 85). Petitioner has not availed herself of the opportunity for a public hearing on the merits of her application.

The other two cases from the United States Court of Appeals for the District of Columbia cited by petitioner as in conflict with the Circuit Court opinion in the instant case clearly evidence no such conflict. Indeed, neither are apposite to the issues here. **Jordan v. United Insurance Company of America,** 289 F. 2d 778, deals with the narrow question whether on the refusal of a certificate of authority to an insurance company the District Court could hold a trial *de novo* or whether such Court was confined to a review of the administrative record. **Minkoff v. Payne et al.,** 210 F. 2d 689, affirmed a holding by the United States District Court for the District of Columbia that the decision of the Alcohol Beverage Control Board to deny renewal of an alcoholic beverage license on the grounds of lack of good moral character of the applicant was proper.

Petitioner contends further that the actions of respondents in the instant case as approved by the decision of the United States Circuit Court of Appeals for the Fifth Circuit are contrary to the principals of procedural due process as previously enunciated by that Court and as stated by this Court.

We submit the record is clear that petitioner was not denied procedural due process. The grant to her on May 6, 1969, of a beer license was only a provisional grant until the minutes of the meeting of May 6, 1969, were approved at the next meeting on May 13, 1969. Until such time, the action of May 6, 1969, could be reconsidered and rescinded. This was in accordance with the City's ordinance, Section 2-17, *supra*. Such action was reconsidered and the license rescinded pending a public hearing on the merits.

There is no suggestion that respondents discriminated against petitioner. Indeed, subsequent to the rescission of her license as aforesaid, petitioner was granted a beer license by respondents at another location (R. 43).

Her forum in the instant case is, we submit, before the appropriate committee and council of the City of Macon and not in this Court.

II

Petitioner contends this Court should review the action of the United States Court of Appeals for the Fifth Circuit in classifying her appeal there as frivolous. Such a proposition would, we submit, require a review by this Court of all such findings by all Circuit Courts of this country. It would, in effect, eliminate this Court's traditional considerations relative to review on writ of certiorari and would make its grant one of right rather than sound judicial discretion.

CONCLUSION

For the reasons stated it is respectfully submitted that the petition for a writ of certiorari should be denied.

JOHN B. HARRIS, JR.
P. O. Address
1200 Georgia Power Building
Macon, Georgia 31201
Attorney of Record for Respondents

Of Counsel

LAWTON MILLER
P. O. Address
501 Georgia Power Building
Macon, Georgia 31201

GERALD S. MULLIS
P. O. Address
305 American Federal Building
Macon, Georgia 31201

Certificate of Service

I, John B. Harris, Jr., counsel of record for the respondents, do certify that I have this date served the petitioner with the Brief of Respondents in Opposition to the Petition for Certiorari by depositing a true copy thereof in a United States mail box with first class postage prepaid, addressed to counsel of record for petitioner, namely, Floyd M. Buford, at his post office address, 165 First Street, Macon, Georgia 31201; and to Manley F. Brown, at his post office address, 549 Mulberry Street, Macon, Georgia 31201.

This 13th day of May, 1970.

John B. Harris, Jr.

Lightning Source UK Ltd.
Milton Keynes UK
UKHW03f0623041018
329996UK00006B/462/P

9 781270 546351